# Mandala
# Abstract Coloring Books

*Copyright: Published in the United States by Beverly Rosa*
*Published December 2016*
*ISBN-13: 978-1541297289*
*ISBN-10: 1541297288*

# Thank you

www.ingramcontent.com/pod-product-compliance
Lightning Source LLC
Chambersburg PA
CBHW051946280526
45789CB00009B/3183